MW01167391

THE
LESBIAN EROTIC:
BAD GIRL
PERSONA
AND OTHER POEMS

SARAH F. PEARLMAN

Copyright © 2013 by Sarah F. Pearlman

ISBN 978-0-7414-9854-0

Printed in the United States of America

Published October 2013

INFINITY PUBLISHING
1094 New DeHaven Street, Suite 100
West Conshohocken, PA 19428-2713
Toll-free (877) BUY BOOK
Local Phone (610) 941-9999
Fax (610) 941-9959
Info@buybooksontheweb.com
www.buybooksontheweb.com

I have to cast my lot with those
who age after age, perversely,

with no extraordinary power,
reconstitute the world.

—Adrienne Rich, "Natural Resources"

Acknowledgements

To the women of the International Women's Studies Institute (IWSI, 1995-2004)—most especially Daphna Amit, Lily Cincone, Mara Keller, and Ellen Boneparth.

Thanks to my writing coach and dear new friend, Toni Amato for suggestions, laughter, and helping to diminish my academic voice.

Jyl Lynn Felman for editing, encouragement, and great conversations.

Alice Fisher for encouragement and reading poems in an early form.

To my beloved grandmother, Eta Bella Schneider Bromberg

—and my family: children and grandchildren who may never read these poems—

and, of course, Gloria Charles.

Contents

Desire

    Bad Girl Persona   7
    Pomegranate   9
    Aegean View   11
    Rough Desire   12
    Sexual Constructions   14
    Two Women   18

Elder Eros

    Bedevilment   23
    Dilemma   25

Legacy

    1941   29
    Kitchen Silence   31

Sorrow

    Anyone Out There   35

Family

    Genealogies   39
    First Granddaughter   43

Pilgrimage

    Two Choruses   48
    Ancestors   51

Notes   55

Desire

I first began to write poetry during the summer of 1995. I had returned to Greece to join the International Women's Studies Institute (IWSI) on Chalki, a tiny island off the coast of Rhodes. Because it was a women's travel group, I assumed that there would be other gay women. However, it didn't take long to discover that I was it— the only lesbian. Once out and saying how lonely I felt, I quickly became the recipient of multiple assurances that being a lesbian wasn't a problem, and because we were all women, "there really wasn't any difference." But there was.

Some women told me they had gay friends; a few confessed that they had slept with women (usually once). It was bad enough being the one lesbian, but it became harder once the focus of the group turned to writing and then performing poetry. Erotic poetry. Feeling increasingly invisible by descriptions of heterosexual intercourse and plunging penises, an idea of a poem began to emerge. At first, a few fragments and then it was like a poem began to write itself—one nearly complete ready for pen and paper—about hot lesbian seduction and sex. No question that I wanted to proclaim the sex in sexual identity, to flaunt sex between women. No question that I wanted to shock.

Performed before a somewhat stunned audience, the poem, *Bad Girl Persona* was a hit. One woman shyly indicated that she might like to sleep with me. A second told me that I had "touched a secret cord," asking what she should do. When a third questioned if I thought she could be a lesbian, I told her there was a waiting list. *Bad Girl Persona* was the first of two erotic poems that I wrote while on Chalki. The second, *Pomegrante* was my response to the assignment of writing a poem about the mythical fruit.

I would not have guessed then that Chalki would be the first of many journeys I would take with the IWSI and that the Institute would become a kind of erotic muse—

6

providing encouragement as well as space for creativity. Nor that I would return to Greece twice more, and over the course of many years travel to Turkey, Australia, Latvia, Lithuania, and Spain to reunion with the women I grew to love, make life-long friendships—and emerge as a writer of erotic lesbian poetry. A most unexpected life turn.

BAD GIRL PERSONA

Hey girl,
I mean
you just gonna love me.

Cause first
I'm gonna
make you laugh,
tell you
my best stories
do my famous
look you
right-in-the-eye
tongue caressing teeth,
sultriest gaze.

Girl,
you gonna just love me.

Get you
on the dance floor
make all
my best moves,
body serpentine
against yours
hips uncoiling
leg sneaks between legs.

Then
I'm takin' you home,
dance all over your body,
do such things
with my mouth
you'll
be beggin' me to stop,
or continue.

And we'll apologize
to neighbors
in the morning,
but not before
I make you
the best cup of coffee
you ever did have.

I mean
girl,

you just gonna love me.

Chalki, Greece
1995

POMEGRANATE

Was it those mythic seeds,
or that glistening
lush
luscious
crimson flesh?
Moist velvet.

Ebony
shades
to shimmering
copper,
cinnamon
thighs
open
tongue slides round
this pomegranate,
no seeds to disturb
tasting
small crevices.

Silken liquid
anoints
joyous mouth
pleasuring
laughing chin.

Chalki, Greece
1995

I fell in love with Greece a long time ago. A stunningly luminous, primordial country. Rounded mountain tops billow against the bluest of skies, waterfalls cascade down glistening rocks forming suggestive crevices, waves softly enter the mouths of coastline caves. A breath-taking landscape of beauty, history, and myth—compressed into one small land. Later, I fell in love with Turkey.

For me, writing poetry is a unique experience. A phrase, a fragment emerges from a place deep beneath thought as if a creative unconscious exists that, once triggered, gradually releases a poetic idea to consciousness. After that, the task is language—pen and paper—seeking words, trying out various sequences, reading aloud until the rhythm feels just right. Then back, finding different words until it is time to say the poem is done, finished. To say goodbye—and leave.

Aegean View emerged while sailing along the Aegina shore. *Rough Desire* during a visit to Ephesus, Turkey.

AEGEAN VIEW

Stone breasts
silhouette
cloudless sky
mountain belly
swells,
then granite thighs
open
to
foam-washed
cleft
spilling
into
many-waved
turquoise sea.

Aegina, Greece
1998

ROUGH DESIRE

Come on
push me down
pin my arms,
you know
the position
mouth hard
tongue fierce
just the right place.

Fingers up me
don't move,
damn bitch
moans
someplace
distant.

Trembling
warmth
invades,
melting
gushes
bathe
grateful
thighs.

Kusadasi, Turkey
2000

Sexual Constructions was a hard poem to write. Elusive. I recall that I first had the idea while traveling in Turkey. I knew what I wanted to say. I wanted to write about Boston's lesbian bar and sexual scene and the changes in lesbian culture across three tumultuous decades—including female-to-male transgender emergence. I wrote some lines, then the first and second parts, and then—blocked, I stopped. Later I went back, gave up, and returned to it many years later. Now it's one of my favorites.

SEXUAL CONSTRUCTIONS

I

In the 70's
takin'
a new woman home
was easy.

Good dope
cheap wine
fall down in bed.

I mean
fall down,
futon on floor
red Indian spread,
incense lit
candles flicker
vibrator plugged in.

Unbutton
flannel shirts,
caress frangipone
or patchouli
between her legs
then mine.

Kay Gardner ready
Moon Circles spinnin'
askin'
what do you
want me to do?
Showin' her
I'm hot, expert
and organic.

In the 70's
takin'
a new women home
was easy.

II

In the 80's
takin'
a new woman home
gettin' harder.

Platform bed
no wine
forget weed
may be in recovery,
talkin' about meetings
tellin' me
what step she's in.

Gets hives from lotion
sneezin' from incense,
sex histories?
Learnin' more
than I ever did
wanna know,
don't matter anyhow
ain't wrappin' no plastic
'round my tongue.

Maybe she vanilla
or a leather wanna be,
tie her up
or hug her to sleep,
take out sex toys
or hide 'em away
don't know if dildoes
are in or out.
I mean
current or passé.

In the 80's
need
two different bedrooms.

In the 80's
takin'
a new woman home
wasn't easy.

III

Takin'
a new woman home
in the 90's
made the 80's
look good.

Don' know who
I'm bringin' home.
Is she a girl?
Was she a boy?

Should I be
puttin' on
my slinky leopard bikini
sleazin' right down her,
or wearin'
loose boxers?

Don' know the music,
put on Kay Gardner
she be sayin'
who in hell is that?
College chicks
talkin' dicks and phalluses
used to think
they were the same.

Been
one long time
since I took
a new woman home.

Boston
2012

For more than 40,000 years the Aborigine of Australia told their stories. Creation stories about the origin of their people and the Australian landscape.

One story describes the emergence of two islands in Jervis Bay near Kangaroo Island—islands that were first called the *Two Sisters* and later the *Pages*. The story is about a husband and his two wives who were caught eating silver bream, a fish forbidden to Aborigine women and punishable by death. The women fled but were followed, caught by their husband, and thrown into Jervis Bay to drown. Sometime later, two islands came into view. Two islands set apart.

I never learned why silver bream and or any other kind of fish were forbidden to Aborigine women. The poem, *Two Women* is my lesbian version. Perhaps a re-telling, one close to the ancient, original—later to be disguised—Aborigine story.

TWO WOMEN

Two women
running
running
scorched desert,
dodging
large rocks
small lizards,
star-shaped leaves
moisten
parched lips.

Two women
running
running,
now
scrub forest
then a lake.

Two women
dance
amidst waves
cook
small fish
on sun-baked stones.

Weary,
hidden by
soft ferns
they sleep
ebony bodies
entwined.

Men crash
through forest
raging curses
terror mute,
first one
then the second
tossed into water
necks broken.

Strong swimmers
foraging
lake bottom
glimpse
two islands
set apart,
yet bound eternally
by coral strands
in endless embrace.

Kangaroo Island, Australia
2001

Elder Eros

While visiting the village of Molyvos on Lesvos—a stunningly beautiful island of olive trees that turn the landscape silver-green—I led a workshop on sex and aging. I wanted to push the idea that lesbian sex and desire doesn't cease with age.

Molyvos is not far from Eressos, the legendary birthplace of Sappho; a mythic homeland where lesbians from all over the world gather. Eressos is a charming, picturesque, and hip village where one can sit for hours in tavernas that line the shore, eat small plates of food or mezes, drink ouzo, and then wade into the warm waters of the Aegean. Both Lesvos and a nearby island, Lemnos are stepping stones to the Turkish coast—once called Anatolia. Mytileni is the capital of Lesvos; Myrina is the major town in Lemnos.

Mytileni and Myrina were sisters. Amazon queens; a myth, a fact that provokes my imagination.

The two poems that follow, *Bedevilment* and *Dilemma*, like many others in this collection, are in "thieved" language—that is, in the African-West Indian dialect of Trinidad, the birthplace of my long-time partner, Gloria Charles. There is simply no way any of this could be said in American-English.

BEDEVILMENT

I old now
an' de devil man afoot,
thievin'
ma desire
stealin'
ma plaisur
takin'
ma sweet wetness
coolin' me down,
make me tired.

Dat devil man
he thievin'
he stealin'
he dryin' me out,
stiffin' ma hips
crampin' ma moves
makin' me ugly
no one wan me.

Legs skinny
belly sag.

Dat devil man
he go thieve
ma desire
stealin'
ma plaisur
stampin' down
ma fire
ceasin'
ma shudder,
silence
ma moan.

Ol' devil man
watch out,
no gonna
bedevil me.

Not over yet.

Molyvos, Lesvos
2004

DILEMMA

I

I'm lookin'
I'm watchin'
eye-ballin' up
eye-ballin' down,
conjurin' her scent
seein'
soft pillow lips
imaginin'
light cocoa
skin
taut
warm silk,
picturin' me
right between those legs.

II

She say, girl
you don' wan' me
you wan' my grandma.

Eyes sharp
gaze cold
I say, girl
I know
she I want.

It's what I can git
is the problem.

Molyvos, Lesvos
2004

Legacy

In 2003, I traveled with the women of IWSI to the Baltic countries of Latvia and Lithuania. On the way from Riga to Vilnius, we visited the forest of Rumbula—a place of absolute horror where in 1941—on November 30th and December 8—at least 26,000 Riga Jews were shot and then buried by German killing squads and their Latvian counterparts.

The first poem, *1941*, is about accompanying my grandmother to synagogue during the early years of World War II and was written as part of an IWSI ceremony of witnessing and remembrance at Rumbula. My mother's family rarely spoke of the war, or what happened to the Jews who had remained in their Ukrainian village. Perhaps they did talk but if they had spoken at all, it would have been in Yiddish, which I do not understand. It was only much later—in 1997 while visiting the Diaspora Museum in Tel Aviv—that I learned how in less than two days during 1943, the remaining Jews, over 2000 in my grandparent's village of Bralivar were shot to death and buried in the mass grave that they themselves had dug.

The second poem, *Kitchen Silence* was written for a poetry class at UMass Boston. I wrote it in reaction to a comment by the teacher that kitchens were the place where family stories were passed on.

1941

A child
a grandmother
walk icy streets
the shul
an old frame house.

Fringed shawls
soiled by years of prayer
the men sway sing-song
heads bent over faded books.

Upstairs, the women cry
a palate of black,
wailing
pierces
sorrow-infused room.

A woman screams,
"mama, mamala"
hurling against
balcony rail.

The women
hold her
wailing become sobs
then,
quiet keening.

The men sway sing-song
heads bent over faded books
the grandmother whispers,
"Luz meir gain ahaim."
"We go home."

Climbing down
stairs creak,
six-year old fingers
clutch callous hands
shul door opens
gray snow glistens.

Riga, Latvia
2003

KITCHEN SILENCE

Apron tied
flour-dusted table
rolling pin in hand
silent kitchen.

My grandmother never told me

what being a Jew was like in her Ukrainian village
or what happened when she fled Russia
at age twenty—a young
woman traveling alone,
making her way thru forests,
across borders—with my mother,
a toddler of two, and my aunt,
then an infant, in her arms.

She never told me

what it was like to cross an ocean
or what happened to the family she left behind
father, brother, cousins
and to learn that all were dead.

I never asked.

Distant radios hum
smatter of Yiddish
no stories here
some things are best
not remembered.

Yeast-scented dough
intricately
braided
now challah.

Small rolls
egg-wash shiny—
cinnamon-sprinkled
sweet round Danish
perfume air.

Oil submerged
rough circles
sugar-dusted
metamorphous
into donuts.

Finally,
dough stretched thin
sugar, cinnamon, raisins, walnuts
the jewel of Shabbos
strudel.

Apron folded
dishes washed
kitchen scrubbed
candles lit,
Shabbos begins.

Saturday mornings
a small grandchild
impatient,
joyously
tastes all.

Silent kitchen
radio hums
smatter of Yiddish,
no stories here
some things are best
not told
or remembered.

Boston
2012

Sorrow

The bonobo are a fascinating species of great apes, and together with the chimpanzee, are our closest living simian relatives. Female bonobos are dominant and have the highest social ranking. Males are subordinate.

Bonobos are playful and relatively unaggressive. Sex is extremely varied (I won't say more, but you can consult the web) and frequently involve same-sex partners. Most interesting is that conflict is resolved through sexual engagement.

Now that's intelligent design.

ANYONE OUT THERE

More chimpanzee
than bonobo
game to amuse
plan gone astray,
or just unintelligent design.

Yet,
a sliver moon
illuminates
night sky
midst travelling stars,
and once arid earth
bursts in bloom
wild flowers
perfume air.

More chimpanzee
than bonobo,
a poor species
deluded
lays waste
to luscious planet,
hormones
profit hold sway.

Game to amuse,
plan gone astray
or just unintelligent design.

Anyone there?

Boston
2012

Family

To Lois, my dearest sister and friend

I am blessed with a family of assorted cultures—Jewish-American, Israeli, West Indian, both Jamaican and Trinidadian—and Portuguese. Mixed-culture families are challenging, often fraught with clash over differences and misunderstandings. Yet they also expand and enrich one's life. Without my West Indian partner, I might have never have known the scent of curry perfuming air, the sensuality of movement, the music of steel drums, dancing behind trucks at Carnival, and witnessing what it is like to live unhurried in present time.

Genealogies was such a fun poem to write.

The second poem, *First Granddaughter*, was requested by Kelsey, my first grandchild who asked that I write a poem about her. Part of being a grandmother is the loss of the right of refusal.

GENEALOGIES

I

Can't say my children
had it easy
traversing terrains
of discord
divorce
maternal adolescence, and
sexual disorientation.

A new world.

I send
my daughter
to alternative schools
where she learns to say,
"fuck you"
and call teachers
by first names.

Age fourteen
she tells me
I can't tell her
nothin'
asks for her allowance.

My son worries
how he'll introduce
a future fiancé.
Punk sister
gay mother
father, encounter
Bly drums groupie
pledged to high
levels of safe disclosure.

II

I call my sister
before eight am
when the rates change,
we complain deliciously
about our children.

My sister calls herself
the Jewish mother
that wasn't.
One daughter
wears khaki to weddings
marries an Israeli man.
My sister says
may he rot
in the bowels
of a kibbutz.

III

Her twins
live in the East Village
have rings
in impossible places
more tattoos
than one can count.

One lives with
a Polish man
the other leaves
a Hungarian boyfriend—
in Budapest.

Our brother's son
marries an Algarve
woman
under a hoopa
of Portuguese lace.

IV

My daughter, she
goes to Jamaica
on vacation
brings back—
a Jamaican.

My granddaughter
well, that girl
calls herself
a Jewmaican.

My son
the strangest of all,
marries a Jewish girl
Long Island family.

V

My sister says
I set the example,
she means
my Trinidad girlfriend.

I say, sister girl
I can cut
one mean mango
drink from coconut shells
not one drop spilled.

My sister
she's not impressed.

VI

My girlfriend,
food like sarasop,
roti, callaloo
and coo coo
inhabit my refrigerator.

In return I make
matzo balls,
teach
the pleasure
of whining.

She reciprocates.

Shows me carnival,
jump behind
steel band trucks.
I tell Jewish jokes
model
how to worry
about money.

She instructs
how to be late.
I reveal
how to push ahead in lines.

She gives me potions
to clean my blood.
I write down names
of Jewish doctors.

My sister says
we are
our family's bad dream.

I say,
we're making
a lot of people Jewish.

Hartford
1997

FIRST GRANDDAUGHTER

Honey-thick halo
frames tiny face
quizzical eyebrows
hover above
black sparkle eyes,
then sweet-spaced teeth.

Kinetic sprite
somersault
handsprings
catapulting
permanently
into my heart.

Hartford
1996

Pilgrimage

Someone will remember us, even in another time

Sappho, 6th century BCE

Many of the Institute women were interested in feminist spirituality and female divinities and while traveling in Greece and Turkey, we participated in rituals in celebration of pre-patriarchal goddesses. Some of us wrote ceremonial pieces that were performed in ancient caves or hillsides that had once been sacred places of goddess worship. Taking the names of favorite goddesses, mine was *Clio* or *Kleio*, the muse of song, dance, history—and poetry.

To some women, goddesses were archetypes. Others rejected male-centered religions, directing gratitude and prayer to a female divine. Still others, more skeptical, joined in for the fun and camaraderie. My own interest was in women-centered cultures that existed long before patriarchy. Over several years, I traveled throughout mainland Greece—as well as Crete and other islands—and much of western Turkey, seeking evidence of ancient or matriarchal civilizations. I found deserted sacred caves, partially excavated Neolithic villages, temple complexes in ruins, vase paintings decorated with lunar symbols—or the labrys— and defaced statues of goddesses. In northern Greece, I came across a wonderful photograph of a goddess, Artemis or Demeter, lifted intact out of the earth.

I wept at Troy without knowing why and at the Delphi museum before a wall engraved with sculptures of slain Amazons, commemorating a victory by the Greeks—and wept again, while traveling by bus through the Olympus mountain passes of central Greece. In the abandoned agora of Izmir, once ancient Smyrna, I was elated to find a majestic statue of Demeter, lifting her marble robe above the vulval triangle between her legs. I didn't have much time. Seeing three men walk towards me, I quickly snapped pictures, and fled.

I visited local museums where small carvings of goddesses were labeled "cult" or "fertility figurines." Then elated, I found a six foot double-headed axe, the labrys, in the Heraklian museum in Crete—and then a sculpted head of Eileithyia, carved in black with features of an African woman. While Knossos is the most tourist-visited site in Crete, it was Eileithyia who was the most revered of ancient earth or birth-giver goddesses. Inspired, I traveled to Amnissos, a village east of Heraklion—once a Bronze-age settlement. Guided by an old man driving a donkey cart, I found Eileithyia's cave, once a sacred place of worship and pilgrimage. One story tells that women would press their bellies against the huge round hill that led to the cave to ensure fertility. Now it was abandoned, strewn with gum wrappers and wilted purple flowers. My visit was short. I made my way back downhill, escorted for a time by a huge bumblebee, the air rarified—mystical— as if a window had opened, only to close again.

Imagine what it must have been like before the waves of warrior tribes entered Greece from the northern steppes. Imagine the flight east across the Aegean to Turkey, or south towards Crete until there was no more escape—east or south. Imagine living in a time when it was understood that freedom and a way of life were ending, that defeat and enslavement were imminent— and that the era of deference to the will and domination of men would soon begin. By 800 BCE, the old matrilineal social order and reverence for women was over; testified to by a new kind of architecture. Houses that once had doors leading to adjoining streets were now constructed around inner courtyards with sequestered women's quarters—an end to access to the larger world—and their own lives.

The first poem, *Two Choruses* was written on the island of Aegina in Greece; the second, *Ancestors* in Konya, a Turkish city near Catal Hoyuk—the largest and most ancient Neolithic settlement to be excavated.

TWO CHORUSES

I

The men speak
voices quiet steel.

We must know our sons,
women
cannot have such freedom,
or they
will be
in every man's bed,
and every women's.

The women speak:

Now is the beginning,
witness honor
life confined
virginity
adultery,
marriage
mock enslavement
name us wives,
father-right prevails.

II

The men speak
voices enraged.

Enough
of goddesses
rituals
processionals
dance,
herbs
potions
that bleed out sons.

We want
to hear
cries
beg in anguish.

The women speak:

Prize bloody sheets
make sons
surrender daughters,
invent doctors
compose illness
call us mad,
pleasure now
abomination
sin.

III

The men speak
voices jagged whispers.

Depart your home
feet bound
face covered
breasts for our amusement
clitoris cut
widows burned.
phallus right is all.

No woman
shall lie
with a women,
we mount them
as we please.

The women speak:

We submit
we obey
we bend
songs mute
dance restrained.

Yet
we wait,
ignorant
or knowing
we wait,
to wait is to survive.

There will be a time
end of
endless winter.

Embracing tall trees
hair streaming
warmed by wind,
we once again
leap to dance
amidst
bright
flowers.

Aegina, Greece
1998

ANCESTERS

I

It gladdens us to know
that you are here.

Bones
you have found
beneath our houses
beads once wound
about strong arms,
small stones
devoutly placed
on hearths
honor the Birth-giver
Mother Goddess.

Yes, it pleases us
to see you.

II

We came
out of forests,
leaving caves
to make homes
near blue seas
close to mountains.

We were first
to know abundance,
grain-covered fields,
fish dancing in nets
trees bent with fruit.

We were first
to plant
first to harvest
first to weave,
singing.

Yes, it pleasures us
to find you.

III

This sweet earth
warm seas,
mountains
yield
melting snow
caress
hillside clefts,
flowers
perfume
fragrant valleys,
stars adorn
half-moon sky.

Yes, with joy
we greet you.

IV

Our celebrations
processionals
were many,
chanting
gratitude
to our beloved
Birth-giver,
strong
drink
brought
visions.

Two women dance
bodies oiled
legs serpentine
coiled,
wound
about each other,

strong fingers
plunge upwards.

Others mount men
drawing them inside
moist earth
wet with dew
opens to seed.

Yes, we smile
to see you.

V

Beloved dead
lay on platforms
open to wind
and air,
birds
feast
then flight,
spilling flesh
and spirit
back to earth.

Bones brought home.

VI

From early times
men were gentle,
then told by
knowing seers
those few born
with warring blood
quickly put to death
leaving
mourning mothers
origin of later myths,
religions.

Except
those who fled
with sons still infants.

Who would
have known,
years later
their return
a brutish people
from the north.

VII

Mountains
cradled us
delaying the destroyers.

We were
not easily subdued,
but no match.
Earth once shared
now owned,
birth-giver male.

Our time
will come again.

Yes, it gladdens us
to see you.

Gladdens us
that you

return.

Konya, Turkey
2000

Notes

Rich, Adrienne. (1978). Resources. *The Dream of a Common Language.* New York: W.W. Norton & Co, 67.

CPSIA information can be obtained at www.ICGtesting.com
Printed in the USA
BVOW03s0623101213

338631BV00007B/199/P

9 780741 498540